THE PASSOVER GOURMET

NIRA ROUSSO

For Esther and Ike Rousso – with love.

THE PASSOVER GOURMET

by

NIRA ROUSSO

KOSHER

ADAMA BOOKS, NEW YORK

Editing: Louis Rousso
Photography: Nelly Sheffer
Photography Styling: Nurit Branizky
Book Design: Tut
Production: Ruth Eilat
Phototypesetting: U.P.P. Ltd. Tel-Aviv
© 1987 Adama Books

ISBN 0-915361-66-3
Adama Books, 306 West 38 Street, New York, N.Y. 10018

Printed in Israel

TABLE OF CONTENTS

INTRODUCTION

In the spring of 1973 I celebrated the Passover Seder outside my parents' home for the first time in my life. We were at my in-laws' home in New York.

The general festiveness and the happy preparations for the holiday were an experience to remember but what remained etched in my memory is the Seder table. The aromas, the varieties and the culinary surprises changed everything I thought I knew about traditional Passover cooking. Here I met Apio – slices of celery root glazed with a sweet and sour sauce. Fritada – the golden-brown pies made with matzah, eggs and vegetables. I first tasted leek patties, layered meat and matzah cakes and a wonderful Haroset unlike any other I tasted before.

All these dishes became permanent members of my Passover kitchen joining the Matzah Brei, the Kneidle and the Chremzel. Since then we have taken to preserving the culinary traditions of many different Jewish kitchens. Our Seder dinner has become the meeting place of these kitchens and the seven days of the holiday are all well celebrated with a long line of brunches and dinners that star Moroccan lamb stew alongside Italian soups. None of our guests has ever complained about the combinations.

The main reason for my writing this book was to prove that cooking on Passover could be as varied as during the rest of the year and did not require any more work. Furthermore, the different Jewish culinary traditions are as much at home with each other as they are with modern kitchen appliances.

The recipes come from many different sources. Some of them travelled a long way to my kitchen from New York, Milano and Rio de Janeiro. Others were just there, a part of my own family's tradition. A large number of recipes are my own adaptations to the delicacies I enjoyed at friends' houses, like the Tunisian fava bean soup, the garlic matzah and the sugar coated matzah from Morocco. A number of these recipes have already appeared in my weekly newspaper column and I selected only those recipes which have become favorites, such as the light Borscht with apples and the meat filled celery roots. I have generally avoided standard salads naturally kosher for Passover, but which any cook could easily devise. Only those salads were selected which in some way typify either the holiday or the season.

My goal was to serve as matchmaker among the different traditions, to show that not only can they be combined but that in fact, they can enhance each other. In so doing there are many fascinating, but not irreverent combinations of old and new. The traditional Fritada coexists comfortably with a broccoli soufflé prepared in a microwave oven.

Special emphasis has been placed on the dessert and baked goods section and a whole chapter has been devoted to brunch and different snacks. There is no reason to forego your favorite dishes in a traditional Passover kitchen, whether it is Pizza, pancakes or bagels. Hopefully, some new recipes will join your old list of favorites.

I hope this book will open a range of new and sometimes unexpected recipes, each deriving in its own unique way from the common, shared Passover traditions of the Jewish kitchens.

Nira Rousso

FROM SCRATCH

HOME MADE HORSERADISH

Yield: 2 cups

1 lb. horseradish
2 beets
2 tsp.salt
1 cup water
½ cup sugar
Juice of 2 lemons

Rinse and peel the horseradish and the beets. Grate on the fine grater of a food processor and transfer to a large bowl.

Add the salt, the sugar and the water. Add salt and sugar to taste. Keep refrigerated.

HORSERADISH SAUCE

Yield: About 2 cups

1 cup herb mayonnaise
(see previous recipe)
½ cup horseradish
2 tbsp. lemon juice
1 tbsp. sugar
1 pinch of salt
¼ cup ketchup

Stir all the ingredients together.

HERB MAYONNAISE

For all the virtues of a food processor it is still more fun to whip the mayonnaise with an egg beater. This old fashioned method allows for better control and for a thicker, creamier texture, in addition to the deliciousness of real mayonnaise enriched with many herbs.

yield: 2 cups

2 egg yolks
½ tsp. salt
2 tbsp. lemon juice
1 tbsp. prepared
mustard
2 tbsp. chopped chives
2 tbsp. chopped dill
2 tbsp. chopped parsley
1 cup vegetable oil

Beat the yolks with the salt until thick and lemony in color. Add the lemon juice, the mustard and the herbs.

Add the oil, very slowly, beating constantly, until the mayonnaise becomes very thick and creamy. This can be done with an egg beater, a manual mixer or an electric mixer. Do not use a food processor.

10

MATZAH STUFFING

Yield: 8 cups

2 onions, diced
4 stalks celery, diced
½ cup margarine
10 matzah, broken
2 cans, 4 oz. each, sliced
   mushrooms, drained.
2 cups chicken broth
1 egg
salt and pepper to taste

Saute the onions, the celery
and the mushrooms in the
margarine until golden. Stir in
the matzah and add the rest of
the ingredients. Let stand for
at least 20 minutes.

HAROSET

*My father's apple–nut Haroset
differs completely from the date
and raisin Haroset served at the
Roussos' Seder table. Yet they are
both equally delicious and,
together with the many varieties
of Haroset from Jewish
communities around the world,
they present a feast worth
preparing and eatin all year
round.*

DATE–APRICOT HAROSET

½ cup pitted dates
2 cups apples, peeled
   and diced
1 cup dried apricots
½ cup chopped walnuts
¼ cup sweet wine

Cook the dates, apples and
apricots together in water to
cover for 15 minutes. Remove
the fruits from the water and
drain well.

Process the fruits with the wine
very briefly in a food processor
until coarsely chopped. Add
the chopped nuts.

11

FROM SCRATCH

ORANGE–WINE HAROSET

¾ cup dark raisins
2 cups pitted dates
Grated peel and juice of
  2 oranges
⅓ cup sweet wine

Process all the ingredients in a food processor, or grind the raisins and the dates in a meat grinder and add the orange peel, the juice and the wine.

GINGER–CINNAMON HAROSET

½ lb. pitted dates
1 ½ cups raisins
2 apples, peeled
½ cup pecans, chopped
1 tsp. ground cinnamon
1 tsp. ground ginger
¼ cup orange juice

Put all the ingredients in a blender or in a food processor fitted with a steel blade and process briefly, until coarsely chopped.

FIG AND COCONUT HAROSET

½ lb. chopped dates
½ lb. dried figs,
  chopped
1 cup grated coconut
1 cup dried apricots,
  diced
1 cup plum preserves
1 tsp. cinnamon
½ tsp. ground cloves
1 cup sweet wine
1 cup chopped pecans

Cook all the ingredients except the pecans, for about 30 minutes, in a covered saucepan. Add small amounts of water, as required.

Remove from the heat and add the nuts.

12

ALMOND–RAISIN HAROSET

4 apples peeled and
  sliced
½ lb. pitted dates
½ cup raisins
2 cups water
½ cup ground almonds
1 cup sweet wine
3 tbsp. lemon juice
Sugar to taste

Put the apples, the dates and
the raisins in a medium
saucepan, add the water and
cook for about 15 minutes.

Strain and coarsely chop the
fruits, add the almonds, the
wine the lemon juice and the
sugar.

BEET PRESERVES (EINGEMACHTS)

Yield: 4 cups

1 ½ cups sugar
1 cup water
2 lbs. beets
Grated peel and juice of
  1 lemon
1 tsp. ground allspice
1 tsp. ground ginger

Cook the sugar and the water
in a large saucepan for 10
minutes.

Peel and grate the beets
coarsely. This can be done with
the coarse grating disc of a
food processor.

Add the beets to the sugar.
Add the lemon juice and peel,
the allspice and the ginger.

Simmer, uncovered, for an
hour on a very low heat. Ladle
into hot, sterilize jars and let
cool.

HOME DRIED APPLES

3–4 lbs. apples (Granny
  Smith or Golden
  Delicious).
½ cup sugar

Peel and core the apples then
slice into rings.

Line a large baking pan with
aluminium foil. Sprinkle the
foil with the sugar and spread
the apple slices on top.

Set the oven at the lowest
possible temperature and let
the apples dry overnight.*

* A nice, old method for
drying apples, is to 'thread' the
apples on a piece of string and
hang the string over a heater or
radiator. The apples will dry
slowly, giving off a wonderful
aroma.

13

BREAKFAST
AND
BRUNCH

QUICK MUFFINS

Prepare them quickly and eat them quickly

Yield: 12 muffins

½ cup milk
½ cup water
⅓ cup butter
½ tsp. salt
1 cup matzah meal
3 eggs
1 tsp. sugar

Preheat the oven to 350° and grease 12 muffin cups.

Heat the butter, the water, the milk and the salt in a large saucepan and bring to a boil. Add the matzah meal, stirring with a wooden spoon.

Continue stirring for 5 minutes and remove from heat.

Add the eggs, one at a time, beating well after each addition.

Add the sugar and let stand for 5 minutes. In the meantime, heat the greased muffin pan in the oven for 5 minutes.

Pour the mixture into the muffin cups and bake for 20 minutes. Lower the heat to 325° and bake for another 15 minutes.

PASSOVER PANCAKES WITH STRAWBERRY SAUCE

Yield: 10 pancakes

1½ cups warm milk
1 cup matzah meal
3 eggs
2 tsp. maple syrup
1 tsp. salt
Oil for frying
Strawberry sauce (See
   below)

Substitute any fresh fruit for the strawberries.

eat the milk and add to the matzah meal. Let the mixture stand for 10 minutes.

Beat the eggs and add to the matzah meal mixture, together with the maple syrup and the salt.

Heat the oil in a frying pan, drop the mixture in by tablespoonfuls, and fry on both sides.

Serve with butter and with strawberry sauce.

STRAWBERRY SAUCE

Yield: 2 cups

1 pint fresh
   strawberries
⅔ cup sugar
1 tbsp. lemon juice
2 tbsp. brandy

This method of preparation enhances the freshness of the fruit because of the very short time of cooking. This simple but very delicious sauce is not limited to pancakes but can be served with crepes and ice creams. Apricots, red plums and peaches can substitute for the strawberries.

ull and rinse the strawberries.

Process the strawberries with the sugar and the brandy until finely chopped in a food processor fitted with a steel blade.

Cook the strawberry puree in a medium saucepan, uncovered, for 5 minutes.

18 Add the lemon juice, and serve warm or cold.

LEEK-FETA PATTIES

A tasty brunch fare from the Sephardic kitchen. Serve with yogurt or with lemon juice.

Yield: 10–12 patties

1 large leek
2 matzah
3 eggs, beaten
5 oz. Feta cheese
½ tsp. ground black
  pepper
Oil for frying

iscard the dark green leaves of the leek, cut the leek lengthwise and rinse thoroughly, dice and parboil in salt water for 10 minutes.

Break the matzah into crumbs and add ¾ cup of the boiling water. Mix well and allow to stand for 5 minutes.

Strain and mash the leek. Add the matzah mixture, the eggs, the cheese and the pepper. Mix well.

Heat the oil in the frying pan, and drop the leek mixture in by tablespoonfuls. Fry until golden–brown on both sides. Drain on paper towels.

Serve warm or cold.

PASSOVER ORANGE GRANOLA

This is my version for an all–time favorite. The Granola is not baked but cooked in a saucepan, and after Passover we replace the Matzah farfel with oatmeal.

½ cup honey
⅓ cup oil
1 cup sesame seeds
1 cup chopped pecans
1 cup chopped almonds
2 cups matzah farfel
½ tsp. cinnamon
1 cup raisins
½ cup grated coconut
Grated peel of 1 orange
¼ cup orange
  marmalade

n a large saucepan, heat the honey with the oil. Add the sesame seeds, the pecans and the almonds and cook in the honey mixture, over medium heat, for 5 minutes, stirring occasionally.

Add the farfel, the raisins, the cinnamon, the coconut, the orange peel and the marmalade, and cook over medium heat for 20 minutes, stirring frequently. Spread the granola on a greased cookie sheet and cool completely.

Store in an airtight container.

MATZAH BREI

The delicate salmon mousse and celery puree of our friend, Rena, have brought her fame and recognition, but it is her very basic and sturdy Matzah Brei, which attracts all of us to her table for Passover brunches. "There is nothing to it" says Rena, except for the taste, of course.

Serves 6

4 matzah
⅔ cup warm milk
3 eggs
½ tsp. salt

Optional: ⅓ cup fried onion
4 tbsp. oil for frying

rumble the matzah into a large bowl and soak them in boiling water for 5 minutes.

Drain and squeeze the matzah, add the warm milk and let stand for 5 minutes.

Add the eggs, the salt and the fried onion.

Heat half the amount of the oil in a large skillet. Add the matzah mixture and fry for 4 minutes.

Slide carefully onto a large plate, add some more oil to the pan and return the large pancake into the pan, to cook on the other side. You may also cut the matzah brei into quarters, while still in the pan, and turn each quarter carefully.

Serve immediately, with sour cream and chives, if the matzah brei includes fried onion. Otherwise, serve with powdered sugar, cinnamon or honey.

SUGAR COATED MATZAH FROM MOROCCO

A lovely Passover treat which kids love. The matzah is first fried and then dipped in a sugar and lemon syrup, for a shiny glaze.

Serves 6

6 matzah
Oil for deep frying

For the syrup:
1½ cup sugar
1 cup water
Juice of 1 medium
  lemon
½ tsp. ground
  cinnamon

Sprinkle the matzah with a little water. Do not soak. Wrap with a damp towel.

Cut each matzah into quarters and deep–fry each piece until golden on both sides. Drain on paper towels.

Cook the sugar, the water and the lemon juice for 30 minutes, uncovered, on medium heat.

Add the fried matzah to the syrup and cook for two minutes more. Remove with slotted spoon, spread the matzah on a tray, sprinkle with some cinnamon and allow to cool.

ITALIAN WALNUT-HONEY GRIDDLE CAKES

Try this Italian sweet version of a Matzah Brei: These griddle cakes are served with honey–lemon syrup, and sprinkled with a bit of nutmeg.

Yield: 15 cakes

½ cup raisins
1 cup sweet red wine
6 matzah
4 eggs, beaten
½ tsp. salt
1 tbsp. grated lemon
  peel
2 tbsp. brandy

½ cup chopped walnuts
Oil for frying
Nutmeg

For the syrup:
¾ cup honey
3 tbsp. water
3 tbsp. lemon juice

oak the raisins in the wine for at least 30 minutes. Drain well.

Soak the matzah in cold water for 20 minutes, drain and squeeze thoroughly.

Mix the matzah with the eggs, the salt, the lemon peel, the brandy, the nuts and the drained raisins.

Heat the oil in a large skillet and drop the mixture in by tablespoonfuls. Fry on both sides until golden–brown.

In the mean time bring the honey, the water and the lemon juice to a boil, and simmer for 4 minutes, uncovered.

Arrange the griddle cakes on a serving platter, pour the syrup over and sprinkle with some nutmeg.

CHEESE TRIANGLES

These mock "Borekas" of Turkish origin, are eaten all year round.

Serves 6

4 matzah
2 medium potatoes,
  cooked
½ cup shredded
  cheddar cheese
½ cup cottage cheese
2 eggs
1 tsp. salt
1 egg, beaten
Oil for frying

oak the matzah in warm water for 5 minutes. Pour the water out carefully, and pat the matzah dry, taking care not to break them.

Mash the potatoes and mix with the cheeses, the eggs and the salt. Do not mix in a food processor, or the mixture might come out too thin.

Cut each matzah into quarters, put a teaspoon of the filling on one side of each piece. Fold the other half over the filling, dip in the egg and fry in hot oil until golden–brown on both sides.

Trim the edges of the fried rectangles into triangles and serve immediately.

שׁוֹמֵר הַבְטָחָתוֹ לְיִ
חִשַּׁב אֶת הַקֵּץ לַעֲ
לְאַבְרָ
פִי הַבְּתָרִים שֶׁנֶּאֱמַר וַיֹּאמֶר אַרְבַּע מֵאוֹ
לְהֶם וַעֲבָדוּם וְעִנּוּ אֹתָם פָרֵשׁ גָּדוֹל
וְכֵן יֵצְאוּ מִכֶּן אֶת

CHEESE ROLLS WITH COCONUT

An Israeli specialty, served at brunch.

Yield: 12 rolls

6 matzah
1 cup Ricotta cheese
2 tbsp. butter, softened
1 egg
Grated peel of 1 lemon
6 tbsp. sugar
1 tsp. vanilla
1 egg, beaten

Margarine for frying
½ cup grated coconut
Confectioners sugar for
  dusting

prinkle the matzah with water, put them one on top of the other, wrap with a damp towel and let stand for 10 minutes.

Mix the cheese, the butter, the eggs, the lemon peel, the sugar and the vanilla.

Cut each matzah in half. Spread 1½ tablespoons of the filling on the long edge of each matzah piece, and roll up jelly–roll fashion.

Dip each roll in the beaten egg and fry in hot margarine on medium heat, until golden–brown on both sides.

Sprinkle the rolls with the coconut and the confectioners sugar.

QUICK PAN-FRIED SPINACH FRITTATA

A short–cut for the Sephardic Fritada. While the traditional Fritada takes an hour to bake in the oven, this wholesome dish is a meal in ten minutes, served with Parmesan and with a green salad.

Serves 4

2 packages (10 oz.
  each) frozen leaf
  spinach
3 matzah
4 eggs, beaten
Salt and pepper to taste
Dash of nutmeg
3 tbsp. margarine
Grated Parmesan

eat the spinach in a saucepan with half a cup of water, until completely thawed.

Strain the spinach, reserving half the amount of the liquid.

Crumble the matzah and pour the spinach and the remaining liquid over them.

Mix thoroughly until the matzah are softened.

Add the eggs, the salt, the nutmeg and the pepper. Heat the margarine in a 12" skillet and add the spinach mixture. Cook on medium heat, uncovered, for 5 minutes on each side. Sprinkle with grated Parmesan and serve immediately.

PASSOVER PIZZA

This pizza comes from Victoria Morhaim, a gourmet cook who teaches Jewish cookery in Peabody, Massachusetts. The very special thing about Vickie is her ability to share her vast knowledge in the form of very clear and methodical recipes.

1 lb. matzah, broken up
Salt and pepper to taste
3 eggs
½ cup oil

For the sauce:
1 large onion
2 cloves garlic
1 can (6 oz.) tomato
  paste

2 cans full of water
1 tsp. basil
Salt and pepper to taste
2–3 cups shredded
  mozzarella

oak the matzah for 10 minutes in warm water and squeeze well. Add the eggs, salt and pepper to taste and the oil. Mix well.

Press the mixture out on a greased pizza pan, leaving a little edge on the sides.

Bake in 350° oven for 30 minutes. This crust can be prepared ahead and frozen.

Saute the onion and the garlic in the oil. Add the tomato paste and the water, season with basil, salt and pepper, Cook for 3 minutes and pour over the crust.

Sprinkle with plenty of grated mozzarella. You may garnish the cheese with mushrooms, olives, pimiento, anchovies or tuna.

Bake in hot oven until cheese is bubbly (about 15 minutes).

33

APPETIZERS AND STARTERS

MEAT FILLED CELERY ROOTS

I published this recipe in my cooking column a couple of years ago. The response was tremendous and apparently it has become a favorite with many families, Ashkenazic and Sephardic alike. The roots, which are at their best in the spring just in time for Passover, are stuffed with a savory filling and then braised in a light lemon–dill sauce.

Serves 8

For the filling:
1 lb. lean ground beef
4 tbsp. oil
1 onion, chopped
2 tbsp. chopped dill

1 tsp. salt
½ tsp. ground pepper
1 egg, lightly beaten
4 large celery roots

For the sauce:
Juice of 1 medium

lemon
½ tsp. salt
2 tsp. sugar
4 tbsp. oil
1 cup water
2 tbsp. chopped dill

eat the oil in a large skillet. Saute the meat together with the onion, the dill, the salt and the pepper for 15 minutes. Stir frequently with a fork.

Peel the celery root, cut into halves, and with a sharp knife, make a well in each half.

Remove the meat mixture from the heat and add the beaten egg. Spoon meat filling into celery halves, and make small balls with the remaining filling.

Place the celery halves in the same skillet in which the filling was cooked and arrange the meat balls and the scraps of celery, which were extracted in the process of making the wells around the celery halves.

Mix all the sauce ingredients, pour over the stuffed celery. Cover and cook over low heat for an hour.

FESTIVE GLAZED CHOPPED LIVER

This very presentable dish enjoys a special flavor acquired by braising the livers in sherry. The addition of unflavored gelatine makes its own glaze.

Serves 10–12

6 medium onions	Salt and pepper to taste	**To garnish:**
2 lbs. chicken livers	5 hard–boiled eggs	Slices of red and green
1 cup dry sherry	1 packet unflavored	peppers, black olives,
4 tbsp. margarine	gelatine	hard–boiled egg.

 n a medium saucepan, heat the sherry, add the livers and braise for 15 minutes, stirring frequently.

Chop the onions and fry them in margarine in a separate skillet until golden brown. Add the livers to the onions and saute for 5 minutes. Season to taste. For the best consistency, grind the mixture with the eggs in a meat grinder.

Soften the gelatine in half a cup of water and add to the liver mixture.

Line the bottom of a loaf pan with a variety of colorful vegetables and slices of egg as a garnish.

Pour the liver mixture carefully over the egg and vegetable slices and refrigerate for 12 hours. The glaze will settle at the bottom.

Before serving, line a long tray with lettuce leaves and slices of pickled cucumbers. Wrap the pan in a warm towel, insert a pointed knife around the edges of the pan and invert the pan over the serving tray.

CAPONATA – AN EGGPLANT-OLIVE DELIGHT

This Italian appetizer is usually served cold. There is an equally tasty hot version in which the Caponata is spread in a baking dish, topped with two beaten eggs and baked for 20 minutes.

Serves 8

1 lb. eggplant
1 tbsp. salt
¼ cup oil (Preferably olive oil)
1 large onion, chopped
3 red peppers, cut into strips
2 garlic cloves, chopped
1 large carrot, peeled
and diced
1 lb. ripe tomatoes, peeled and diced
1 cup green olives, pitted and cut in half
3 tbsp. wine vinegar
2 tbsp. sugar
1 tbsp. dried basil
2 tbsp. chopped dill

eel the eggplant, cut into cubes and sprinkle with salt. Let stand for 30 minutes.

Pat the eggplant pieces dry with a paper towel.

Heat the oil in a large saucepan; add the eggplants and simmer for 10 minutes uncovered, on a high heat, stirring frequently.

Add all the other ingredients, lower the heat, cover and simmer for 40 minutes.

Chill and serve as an appetizer. The Caponata may also be served warm.

HUEVOS HAMINADOS (BROWN EGGS)

These tasty eggs are a common favorite in many Jewish communities, ranging from the Mediterranean and Balcan versions to the remote cuisines of Buchara and Georgia. My uncle from Tashkent used to cook them for several hours and then he would peel and braise them slowly in onions, olive oil and spices. I can still smell them to this day. I have never succeeded in watching my mother in law, Esther Rousso, prepare them, she does it so fast. But they are delicious. We serve these brown eggs for a Sunday breakfast or brunch. Eating them is a ritual: The eggs are peeled and cut into quarters. Salt and pepper are added carefully and fresh lemon is squeezed slowly over the eggs. At a Sephardic brunch, the eggs usually accompany a "fritada" of spinach, leek or Swiss chard, whichever is in season.

I cook them in a pressure cooker. All three methods are described here.

BROWN EGGS, TASHKENT STYLE

10 large eggs
1 onion, chopped
¼ cup olive oil
½ tsp. salt
½ tsp. ground pepper

Parboil the eggs in water to cover for 10 minutes. Lower the heat, cover and cook the eggs for about 3 hours.

Remove the eggs from the water and crack the shells, without actually peeling the eggs.

Heat the onion in the olive oil, add the eggs, salt and pepper.

Braise, uncovered on a low flame, for 1½ hours. Serve plain or with lemon juice.

ESTHER ROUSSO'S METHOD:

Boil 10 eggs in water to cover for 10 minutes. Reduce the flame and add salt.

Onion skins are added to colour the egg shells a deep brown. Cover and cook for 4 hours.

Serve with salt, pepper and lemon wedges.

PRESSURE COOKER METHOD

Put 10 eggs in a pressure cooker, cover with water and bring to a boil, uncovered. Parboil for 5 minutes. Add water to cover, seal with the lid and cook for 1 hour after pressure has been built. Remove from heat but leave the lid on for another 15 minutes. Reduce pressure according to manufacturer's directions.

42

PINEAPPLE-HORSERADISH SALAD

This Passover version includes celery, horseradish and walnuts, which all characterize the holiday. It is an ideal salad for the Seder meal.

Serves 6

3 celery stalks
2 large apples, peeled
1 can crushed pineapple
1 cup walnuts
½ cup mayonnaise
2 tbsp. lemon juice
2 tbsp. sugar
2 tbsp. horseradish

ice the celery, grate the apples and mix all the ingredients.

Chill and serve in wine goblets.

MATZAH-CHICKEN TURNOVERS

A popular Israeli dish, served with herbed mayonnaise. (See recipe.)

Yield: 10 turnovers

5 matzah
1 large onion
2 tbsp. oil
1½ cups ground cooked
  chicken
3 eggs, divided
2 tbsp. matzah meal
Salt and pepper
Oil for frying

Sprinkle the matzah with water and wrap them with a damp towel. Let stand for 10 minutes.

Chop the onion and saute in the oil until golden. Add the chicken and cook for 10 minutes. Remove from heat.

Add two eggs and the matzah meal and season to taste. Cut each matzah in half. Near the narrow edge of each half, put a tablespoonful of the chicken mixture and roll the matzah carefully.

Dip each roll in the remaining beaten egg and fry in hot oil or margarine until golden–brown on both sides.

PIQUANT CHEESE CANAPES

Yield: 12

6 matzah
2 eggs
1 cup (¾ lb.) shredded
   sharp Cheddar cheese
½ cup cottage cheese
2 oz. margarine,
   softened
2 heaping tbsp. matzah
   meal

1 tsp. mustard
Salt to taste
Paprika to taste
Oil for frying
1 cup shredded
   Emmental or Swiss
   cheese

Sprinkle the matzah with water and wrap them in a damp towel. Let stand for 10 minutes.

Separate the eggs. Combine the sharp Cheddar with the cottage cheese, margarine, egg yolks, matzah meal, salt, paprika and mustard.

Beat the egg whites until soft peaks form.

Cut each matzah in half. Put a tablespoon of the cheese mixture near the narrow edge of each half and roll up carefully.

Dip each roll in the egg whites and fry in hot oil until golden–brown on both sides.

Drain on paper towels, place in a small heat–proof serving dish, top with the Swiss cheese and broil for a few minutes until cheese is melted and bubbly.

MUSHROOM MEATBALLS WITH HERBS

Serves 6

1 lb. lean, ground meat
1 tbsp. dried
   mushrooms
1 large onion, chopped
2 tbsp. chopped dill, or
   2 tsp. dried dillweed
2 tbsp. chopped parsley
1 tbsp. chopped thyme
   or 1 tsp. dried thyme
   leaves
1 egg
1 matzah, crumbled
½ tsp. salt
½ tsp. pepper
3 tbsp. maragrine
1 can (10¾ oz.)
   condensed chicken
   broth
2 tbsp. dried
   mushrooms

 ix the meat, 1 tbs. of dried mushrooms, onion, herbs, egg, matzah, salt and pepper with a wooden spoon.

Form balls with wet hands, and fry them in the hot margarine until golden both sides.

Add the chicken broth and two tbs. of the dried mushrooms and simmer the meat balls for 30 minutes.

Garnish with chopped dill and serve immediately.

ONION DUMPLINGS WITH PRUNES

These dumplings are stewed in a sweet and sour dark prune sauce with honey. It is a real treat, believed to originate in the Litvak Jewish cooking tradition.

Serves 6

2 cups boiling water
2 tbsp. oil
1⅓ cup matzah meal
1 grated onion
3 eggs, beaten
Salt and pepper to taste

15 prunes
2 cups water
2 tbsp. margarine
2 tbsp. honey

o the boiling water add the oil, matzah meal, onion, eggs, salt and pepper and mix well. Chill in the refrigerator for 2 hours.

In a large saucepan, cook the prunes in water with the margarine and honey for 15 minutes.

Form dumplings with wet hands, add them carefully to the simmering prunes. Cover and cook for 40 minutes.

This dish can also be cooked in a pressure cooker. Simmer the prunes for 5 minutes after the pressure has built up, then add the dumplings and cook for an additional 15 minutes with pressure.

WALNUT-ONION SALAD (MOCK CHOPPED LIVER)

Serve this nutritious, vegetarian dish plain with sliced eggs or on a bed of lettuce leaves. It can also be used to stuff tomatoes.

Serves 4–6

2 onions, chopped
6 tbsp. oil
1½ cups chopped
   walnuts
5 hard boiled eggs
1 tsp. sugar
Salt and pepper to taste

ry the onions in the oil with the sugar until golden brown. Remove the onions from the skillet with a slotted spoon and set aside.

Fry the walnuts in the skillet for 1 minute. If the onions absorb all the oil, add a little more oil.

Remove the walnuts with a slotted spoon. Grind the onions, walnuts and eggs together in a meat grinder or in a food processor fitted with a steel blade and season to taste. Refrigerate.

SHAKSHOOKAH

The Shakshookah is a kind of stew, consisting of various vegetables in a tomato sauce, in which eggs are poached. Tunisian in origin, it is a big favorite in Israeli kitchens. It is considered a somewhat "humble" dish, intended to satisfy the hungry members of one's family, rather than impress dinner guests. I find this simple combination very colorful and tasty. On one occaision I served it to friends in Boston and their happy approval has made this a regular part of my guest menu ever since.

There are many variations for a Shakshookah: The vegetables in the stew vary according to season but will always include tomatoes and onions. The eggs are sometimes poached whole and sometimes beaten and poured over the simmering vegetables forming an "omelette" served in its own cooking juices.

Serves 6

4 tbs. oil
1 large onion, sliced
3 ripe tomatoes, sliced
1 red pepper, cut into
  strips

2 cloves garlic, chopped
1 small can tomato
  paste
1 cup water
Salt and pepper to taste
6 eggs

eat the oil in a medium saucepan, add the onions, tomatoes, pepper and garlic, and saute for 5 minutes.

Add the tomato paste and water, bring to a boil and season to taste with salt and pepper.

Make a well in the simmering vegetables and drop a whole egg inside. Repeat the process with the remaining eggs. Cover and poach the eggs for 10 minutes on a medium heat.

Serve 1 egg on each plate, topped with the vegetables and the tomato sauce.

וּמֵת כָּל־בְּכוֹר בְּאֶרֶץ מִצְרַיִם – – – וְהָיְתָה צְעָקָה גְדֹלָה בְּכָל־אֶרֶץ מִצְרַיִם (שמות יא.
מִקֻּנְהוֹת מִצְרִיּוֹת, מִקֶּבֶר הַכֹּהֵן וְסֶרַחַת, נָא־אָמוֹן, שְׁנַת 1500 לִפְנֵי לַסְּפִירָה.

FISH

FISH PATTIES

Use a large pot since the patties puff up during the cooking.

Yield: app. 25 patties

4–5 lbs. carp and
  whitefish
5 eggs
2 large onions
2 carrots
1 tsp. salt
½ tsp. ground pepper
1 tbsp. sugar
Dash of ground nutmeg
Fish stock (See recipe)

Remove the fish from the bones. Use the bones and the heads for the fish stock.

Grind the fish, the onions and the carrots. Mix with all the other ingredients. It is preferable to work on the mixture with the kneading hook of a mixer. The longer you beat, the fluffier the patties will be.

Heat the fish stock to a boil. In the meantime form patties with damp hands. Add the fish patties to the pot.

Cook for 1½ hours in a slowly simmering stock. Add water as required. For a rich aspic, add a smaller amount of water.

Chill, garnish with carrots and with the jellied fish stock.

BASIC FISH STOCK

Yield: 6 cups

Heads and bones of 2–3
  carps or other fish
1 celery root, peeled
  and cut up
2 onions, cut up
1 sprig parsley
1 sprig dill
3 carrots, cut up
1 leek, cut up
1–2 tsp. salt

Rinse the fish and put in a large pot with all the vegetables and the salt.

Cover with water, bring to a boil, cover, lower the heat and cook for an hour. (20 minutes in a pressure cooker).

Strain and season to taste.

SOLE AGRISTADA

The Agristada sauce for fish is characteristic of the excellence of the Sephardic cuisine. Take very simple ingredients, such as lemon and eggs and dill, combine them in the magic Sephardic way and enjoy an exquisite gourmet dish. My husband's grandmother, Calie Morhaim, cooked the tastiest fish Agristada. Here is her recipe.

Serves 4

4 filets of Sole, (about 2 lbs.)
Juice of 1 lemon
1½ cups water
Salt and pepper to taste
2 tbsp. oil

For the Agristada sauce:
3 eggs
Juice of 1 lemon, mixed with:
1 tbsp. potato starch
2 tbsp. chopped dill
Additional chopped dill or parsley to garnish

Sprinkle the fish with the lemon juice and let stand for 30 minutes.

In a large saucepan, put the fish, the water, the salt, the pepper and the oil. Bring to a boil and cook, covered, for 8 minutes. Lift the fish out carefully so as not to break them and put on a serving platter.

Beat the eggs in a bowl, add the lemon juice–potato starch mixture and continue beating. Add half a cup of the cooking liquid to the egg mixture and mix well.

Return the fish stock to the heat. Slowly add the egg mixture and the dill and beat vigorously until the sauce thickens but before it comes to a boil.

Remove from the heat and pour over the fish. Garnish with chopped dill or parsley and serve lukewarm or cold.

SEA BASS IN SABRA AND ALMONDS

The fish is baked in white wine and acquires a special aroma from the Israeli orange liqueur. Another orange liqueur may be substituted for the Sabra.

Serves 6

6 sea bass steaks (about
  3 lbs.)
½ cup (1 stick) butter
1 cup dry white wine
4 tbsp. Vermouth
2 tbsp. Sabra or orange
  liqueur
2 tbsp. soy sauce
1 tsp. freshly ground
  black pepper
1 cup blanched almonds

reheat the oven to 350°.

Arrange the fish steaks in a heatproof baking dish and dot with the butter. Bake for about 20 minutes.

Mix the wine, Vermouth, Sabra, soy sauce and pepper and pour over the fish. Bake for another 30 minutes.

Garnish with the almonds and serve immediately.

CARP-HORSERADISH PATTIES

An interesting variation of Gefilte Fish, and an ideal dish for the second Seder.

Yield: 20 patties

4 lbs. ground carp
1 onion, minced
2 eggs, beaten
1 hard boiled egg,
  chopped
2 tbsp. white
  horseradish
1 tbsp. sugar
1 tsp. salt
Basic fish stock (see
  recipe)

ix all the ingredients and set aside. Prepare the fish stock and bring to a boil.

Form fish patties with wet hands. Slide the patties gently into the boiling stock, cover and cook for 30 minutes. Remove patties from stock with slotted spoon, cover and refrigerate patties and stock.

Arrange the patties on a serving platter. Garnish with the jellied fish stock, with sprigs of parsley or with red horseradish. Serve cold.

63

STEAMED BACALA WITH VEGETABLES

A low–calorie dish with an oriental flavor.

Serves 6

6 portions of Bacala
½ tsp. salt
½ tsp. ground ginger
½ tsp. freshly ground
  pepper
1 celery root, peeled
  and diced
1 small leek, cut into
  rings
1 red pepper, cut into
  rings
3 carrots, sliced
2 scallions, cut into 1–
  inch pieces
1 tbsp. soy sauce
Few drops of sesame oil
  (optional)

lean the fish and rub with the salt, the ginger and the pepper.

Line a steamer or a colander with a damp cheese cloth. Put all the vegetables on the cheese cloth and arrange the fish on top. Sprinkle the vegetables with salt.

If a colander is used for the steaming, put it in a very large saucepan filled with 2 cups of boiling water. Cover and steam the fish and the vegetables for 30 minutes.

Adjust the seasoning, add the soy sauce and a few drops of Sesame oil, and serve immediately.

SWEET AND SOUR CARP

Serves 6-8

3 lbs. Carp, cut into
  steaks
1 onion, sliced into
  rings
1 red pepper, cut into
  strips
1 green pepper, cut into
  strips
1 can (8 oz) crushed
  pineapple

1 cup pineapple syrup
1 tsp. ground ginger
3 tbsp. lemon juice
⅓ cup sugar
1 tsp. salt
⅓ cup white wine
¾ cup pineapple juice
1 tsp. potato starch,
  diluted in a little water
Sliced pineapple for garnish

Put the fish, the onion, the pepper and the pineapple in a large pan.

Combine the ginger, the lemon juice, the sugar, the salt and the wine and pour over the fish and the vegetables.

Add the pineapple juice and cook, uncovered, for 30 minutes.

Remove the fish gently from the pan and transfer to a serving dish.

Cook the remaining sauce and vegetable for another 5 minutes.

Add the starch, diluted with water and cook until the sauce thickens slightly.

Pour the sauce over the fish, garnish with pineapple slices and serve.

TROUT WITH PINE NUTS AND WALNUTS

Serves 6

2 large trouts, about 1½
  lb. each
½ cup fine matzah meal
2 tbsp. oil
½ cup walnuts, coarsely
  chopped
2 oz. pine nuts
½ cup white wine
⅓ cup celery leaves
Salt and pepper
2 tbs. butter

Clean the trouts, dip in the matzah meal and brown lightly in the oil on both sides.

Make a cut lengthwise in the trouts. Mix the walnuts and the pine nuts, divide the mixture in half and stuff the trouts with half of the nut mixture. Reserve the remaining nut mixture.

Arrange the trouts in an oven proof dish. Combine the celery leaves, the white wine, the salt and the pepper and pour over the fish.

Cover the dish with aluminium foil and bake at 350° for 30 minutes.

Lightly toast the remaining half of the nut mixture in 2 tablespoons of butter. Put on top of the baked fish and serve immediately.

TUNA CROQUETTES IN LEMONY TOMATO SAUCE

Another Turkish Jewish favorite; Very ordinary ingredients which are combined in a sophisticated method to make a gourmet dish.

Yield: 10 croquettes

2 cans Tuna, (10 oz
  each) packed in water
¼ cup matzah meal
2 eggs, beaten
2 tbsp. chopped parsley
1 grated onion
Salt and pepper
Oil for deep frying

For the sauce:
3 tbsp. lemon juice
1 cup water
1 large tomato, crushed
1 tsp. sugar
Salt and pepper

rain and flake the Tuna. Add the matzah meal, the eggs, the parsley, the onion, the salt and the pepper. Form balls with wet hands.

Heat the oil and fry the croquettes, a few at a time, until golden brown on both sides.

In a small saucepan, mix all the sauce ingredients and bring to a boil.

Serve the croquettes hot, with the warm sauce on the side, or chill the croquettes in the sauce, and serve as an appetizer.

לחיי העולם הבא מגדיל ישען

מלכו ועושה חסד למשיחו לא

דוד ולזרעו עד עולם עושה שלום

במרומיו הוא יעשה שלום עלינו

ועל כל ישראל ואמרו אמן

ועל כל ישראל ואמרו אמן

חזק ונתחזק... כפירים רשו

רבי

אשר

המפלבות

שב

SOUPS, NOODLES, DUMPLINGS

f. 30b

LIGHT BORSCHT WITH APPLES

Serve this light soup drink chilled, over ice, in a glass pitcher.

Serves 10

3 lbs. beets, peeled and
  sliced
5 cups water
2 cups tomato juice
2 tbsp. sugar, or to taste
2 tbsp. lemon juice
1 tsp. salt
1 cup apple juice
2 apples, peeled and
  diced

Lemon wedges or
  pineapple slices for
  garnish

rate the beets with the grating disc of a food processor and cook with the water, the tomato juice, the sugar, the lemon juice and the salt for 30 minutes, in a large, covered saucepan.

Strain the soup, let cool and add the apple juice and the diced apples. Taste and correct the seasoning. Add sugar or artificial sweetener according to taste.

74   Serve with lemon wedges or with pineapple slices.

BROCCOLI–OLIVE–BASIL SOUP

In the village where I live, we have a Gourmet Club, in which people get together every month or so and sit down for a festive meal. The 160 participants are divided into groups of eight. Each couple is responsible for two dishes. The meal and the sharing of labor are planned in advance and every meal samples another cuisine.
I have developed this recipe for the Northern Italian meal which took place on Passover and we ate it with Garlic Matzah. Both recipes are given here.

Serves 8–10

3 tbsp. margarine
1 onion, grated
1 lb. frozen broccoli,
  thawed and squeezed
10 green olives, pitted
  and chopped

1 potato, grated
1 sprig parsley
2 tbsp. dried basil
Salt and pepper
6–7 cups water
1 egg

Grated Parmesan cheese

eat the margarine in a soup pot, add the onion and saute until golden brown.

Add the broccoli, the olives, the potato, the parsley, the basil, the salt, the pepper and the water. Bring to a boil. Cover, lower the heat and cook for 30 minutes or until the broccoli is soft.

Remove and discard the parsley.

With a slotted spoon transfer the cooked vegetables into a food processor, add the egg and process very briefly, until coarsely chopped.

Return the vegetables to the pot, taste and correct the seasoning and cook for 5 more minutes.

Serve with grated Parmesan cheese and with Garlic Matzah.

GARLIC MATZAH

Try this idea to bring new life to any vegetable soup. The following basic quantities can be multiplied.

Serves 4

2 matzah
Pinch of salt
4 tbsp. olive oil
4 cloves garlic
2 tbsp. water

Sprinkle the matzah with a little water and with some salt. Let stand for 5 minutes.

In the meantime put the oil, the garlic cloves and the water in a food processor fitted with a steel blade and process into a thin paste.

Cut the matzah into four. Brush each piece with the garlic paste, broil for 1–2 minutes or until the garlic matzah are golden. Serve hot.

FAVA BEAN SOUP FROM TUNIS

Fresh green fava beans are at their peak during the early spring days of Passover. The Moroccan and Tunisian Jews enjoy them in a large variety of delectable Passover dishes, from the well loved lamb and fava bean stew to many versions of soups and accompaniments. Fresh fava beans are tender and the peel comes off easily. This version of soup uses canned fava beans. The preparation is quick and easy with no sacrifice of the traditional taste.

Serves 8

1 can (16 to 20 oz) fava
  beans
2 potatoes, diced
2 onions, sliced
1 carrot
2 celery stalks
Salt and pepper

1 can (6 oz) tomato
  paste
1 lb. beef shank, cut up
1 tsp. ground cumin
7 cups water
Crushed red pepper or
  hot pepper sauce

ut aside half the amount of the beans. These will be added to the soup at the final stages of the cooking.

Put the remaining amount of the beans, together with the canning liquid in a blender or a food processor and puree thoroughly.

Put all the ingredients, except for the whole beans, in a large pot and cook for an hour and a half. Add the whole beans and cook them in the soup for two minutes.

Taste and correct the seasoning. This soup requires a certain degree of spiciness and crushed hot peppers or a hot pepper sauce are a welcome addition.

CREAM OF ARTICHOKE SOUP

Passover is the most appropriate time to enjoy this dish. I like to think that I invented it, but I'm sure that someone has already come up with the same idea. The special flavor is obtained only by cooking fresh artichokes, which are at their best in the spring. This involves a certain amount of work, but the results are well worth it.

Serves 6

4 large artichokes
4 tbsp. butter
1 small leek thinly
  sliced

1 small parsnip, peeled
  and diced
4 cups water
½ tsp. ground nutmeg

Salt and pepper to taste
1 cup light cream or
  half and half
Chopped parsley and
  chives for garnish

 ut the stems off the artichokes. Using sharp scissors, snap off the outer leaves, down to the white, meaty part. Using a sharp knife, trim the center cone, down to the white base. Scrape away all the fuzzy "choke" and rinse thoroughly.

Another method for trimming the artichoke is to cut off the outer leaves and then cook the artichoke in boiling water for 30 minutes. The leaves and the fuzz will come off easily, but some of the taste will go.

Heat the butter in a soup pot and saute the leeks for 7 minutes. Add the parsnip.

Cut the trimmed artichokes into large strips. Add to the soup with the water. Add salt, pepper and nutmeg.

Bring to a boil, cover and cook for 40 minutes.

Puree the cooked vegetables and return to the pot. Cook for another 5 minutes and correct the seasoning.

Before serving, add the light cream, heat briefly and garnish with chopped parsley and chives.

CHICKEN–LEEK VICHYSSOISE

Serves 8

1 large leek
1 large potato
4 tbsp. margarine
2 tbsp. chopped dill
1 lb. chicken parts,
   wings, necks and back
   bones
Salt and pepper
6 cups water
1 cup parve cream
Additional leek, sliced
   for garnish

 inse the leek thoroughly and remove the dark green leaves. Cut the white and the light green parts into rings.

Peel and dice the potato. Saute the leek in the margarine for 7 minutes, stirring frequently.

Add the potato, the dill, the chicken parts, the salt and the pepper. Add the water and cook for 40 minutes. (15 minutes in pressure cooker.)

Remove the chicken bones from the soup. Mash the vegetables in the soup, correct the seasoning, add the pareve cream and cook for two more minutes.

Garnish with fresh leek slices.

SPRING CHICKEN SOUP

A perfect stage for all the dumplings, the noodles, the egg drops and the kneidlach.

Serves 8

1 small chicken, cut up
1 small red pepper,
  seeded
2 carrots
1 onion
1 small celery root with
  leaves
1 small leek
1 sprig of parsley
1 sprig of dill
Salt and pepper
Water

rim the excess fat from the chicken and reserve for other use.

Peel and slice the vegetables and put all the ingredients in a large soup pot. Cover with water (about 8 cups) , bring to a boil, cover and cook for 1 hour on low heat.

Serve with one of the following suggestions for Passover soup accompaniments.

POTATO EGG–DROP SOUP

The egg drops are enriched with grated potato, to thicken the soup.

Serves 6

6 cups Spring Chicken
　Soup (see preceding
　recipe)
1 small potato, cooked
3 eggs, beaten
½ tsp. salt
1 tsp. potato starch
3 tbsp.
Chopped parsley for
　garnish

eat the soup to boiling.
In a food processor fitted with a steel blade,
process the potato, the eggs, the salt and the
potato starch.

When the soup is near boiling, drop the mixture in by
teaspoonfuls. The drops are ready when they float to the
surface.

Garnish with chopped parsley and serve.

AVGOLEMONO (EGG–LEMON) SOUP

A traditional Passover soup in Jewish communities of Greek and Turkish origin.

Serves 6

5 cups Spring Chicken
  Soup, strained
½ cup matzah farfel
1 egg
Juice of ½ lemon
Salt and pepper

eat the soup in a pot together with the farfel until the soup is boiling and the matzah farfel is very tender.

In a separate bowl, beat the egg with the lemon juice until smooth. Gradually add 1 cup of the hot soup to the egg mixture, whisking vigorously.

Return the egg mixture to the soup, heat for 1 minute, stirring constantly to prevent the egg from settling.

Adjust the seasoning and serve.

PASSOVER EGG NOODLES

Serves 6

4 eggs, beaten
4 tbsp. potato starch
1 cup water
Pinch of salt
Fat for frying

eat the eggs with the potato starch, the water and the salt in a blender or a food processor to make a smooth batter.

Refrigerate the batter for at least 30 minutes

Grease an 8" skillet and heat. Add about 3 tbsp. of the batter.

Tilt the pan so that the batter covers the botton evenly. Cook for 1 minute.

Repeat the procedure with the rest of the batter. The pan must be greased several times in the beginning, for each "crepe" but as it heats through, no further greasing is required.

Put the crepes one on top of the other and cut into noodles.

POTATO DUMPLINGS

4 potatoes, peeled
1/4 cup oil
4 eggs, beaten
4 tbsp. potato starch
1/2 tsp. salt

A recipe of Sarah Schwebel. These dumplings are served with soups and bouillons, or tossed in butter or margarine and served as a side dish. For a heart–pleasing dairy dish, heat the dumplings in butter and serve with fried onions and sour cream.

ook the potatoes in water to cover until soft. Drain and allow to cool.

Mash the potatoes with the oil, the eggs and salt. This is better done by a potato masher. Add the potato starch and refrigerate for an hour.

Dust a work surface with some potato starch and roll out the potato mixture.

Fill a large pot with water, add 1 tbsp. of coarse salt and bring to a boil.

Cut into small squares with a pasta cutter or with a sharp knife. Cook the dumplings in the boiling water until they float up to the surface.

RICH MATZAH BALLS

3 egg yolks
1 cup lukewarm water
1 tsp. salt
2 tbsp. margarine, melted
1 tbsp. parsley, finely chopped.
1 1/4 cup matzah meal
3 egg whites

eat the egg yolks and mix them with the water, the salt, the margarine and the parsley.

Add the matzah meal gradually. Beat the egg whites until stiff peaks form and fold them into the mixture.

Refrigerate for 2 hours. Form balls with wet hands and cook them in boiling chicken soup or beef bouillon.

VICKIE'S TOASTED FARFEL

Take broken matzah, add some water and some salt, toast in a bit of oil and end up with a golden–brown treat that kids and adults cannot resist. Another wonder of the Sephardic kitchen, which we practice in our kitchen for every holiday.
Use egg matzah for a richer variation.

4 matzah
½ cup boiling water
1 egg, beaten
½ tsp. salt
4 tbsp. oil

Break the matzah, mix with the water and squeeze dry.

Add the salt and the egg. Heat the oil in a large frying pan until it sizzles when a small piece of matzah is added.

When the oil is very hot, add the broken matzah and stir constantly. Continue the stir–frying on a medium heat, so that the farfel are toasted evenly. After 10–15 minutes the farfel will be golden–brown and very crisp.

Serve with soup or as a side dish.

CHICKEN DUMPLINGS

These rich, tiny dumplings come from Italy.

Yield: 20 dumplings

Breast of 1 chicken,
  skinned and boned.
1 egg, beaten
¼ cup matzah meal
½ tsp. salt
Dash of nutmeg
Chicken soup

rind the chicken and mix with the egg, the matzah meal, the salt and the nutmeg. Refrigerate for at least 20 minutes.

Bring the chicken soup to a boil. Form tiny balls and drop into the soup. Cover and cook for 20 minutes.

ווי אז מן הוט די חרימן יודן קומן אויז איר לעבן:

פירוש צלי אש

ותשל
כמ

וידע אלהים יודע את מן הקל
מלאח יודע את חנה לדרום
אסתני אלהים נס כי תמאים
ידע יודע כי אין אדם יודע
הקטה ואמתני מבין אדם כי
אס האלהים

ואת עמלנו

בסתר לאכ
להעליב לי
שתצוד
כי חרפה מפורסמ ו
מחה דת שהיו עושים
העמל ובנדלס
במהרים ואת
המכדרים הכ

ונצעק

אול מיר מירחן
גוט מרחן
אול עד הורט גמ
פטוס אול עד ע
די
פייר אונ' אוכר תש
אול אוכר תטמון

וישמע

את יה
אומר
דער פסוק נש
הורט ע
אול עד

פסוק זאגנט
מאלכט ערטיש
מצרים קינדר ישראל
הערטיגליך:

ונצעק

אול

בורדרן' אז דש
זאגנט אול עם חל
דען שאנן זיק מך
זעלביגן אול ש
מצרים אונ' אוט וש
קינדר ישראל ם
דיכשט אול זא...
עם גוט דש חש

וישמע

ויעבידו מצרים את בני ישראל בפרך: ויהי
כמה שנאמר ויעבידו מצרים וימת מלך שועתם
אל יי' אלהי אבותינו
בימים הרבים מן העבודה' ויזעקו ותעל אל יי' אלהי אבותינו
ואנחנו בני ישראל מן העבודה' ונצעק אל עמלינו ואת
אל האלהים מן העבודה' וירא את ענינו ואת
וישמע יי' את קולנו וירא לחצינו'
את קולנו כמה שנאמר וישמע אלהים את נאקתם ויזכור אלהים את יעקב
וישמע את נאקתם ויזכור אברהם את יצחק ואת כמה שנאמר
את ארץ

הכתוב
בכורים
ויהי בימי
אכחו ויסעק
ולא כמתרב
מעצמו
עפרים וחילי
ולבם ככוו
מלך לה יתהכד
תפלה מה סממע
ונו' לא היה בעדם לבד
כמ'ש ויחמר אלהים
ברס כי תמובת וחמלתם
כות ההוא החוה לא היתה
הברית הגאולה:
מספרת ביאר מהעמקי
והלחן הנאת
מסבירת הגדולה:
ובאר מהעב
אויו חיו לם ויעבוכו ויתנו
כמא' מאל חלל וגל ירד
ברירתו ויזעכו ויתן
הברית ההוא ויד... מצרים
וירא

MEAT AND POULTRY

STUFFED CHICKEN IN COFFEE GLAZE

Serves 8

For the stuffing:
2 matzah, broken
1 large onion, chopped
3 tbsp. margarine
1 large potato, grated
2 eggs
2 tbsp. matzah meal
1 tbsp. parsley,
  chopped
½ tbsp. salt
½ tbsp. pepper

2 – 3-lbs. whole broiler–
  fryer chickens
2 tbsp. soy sauce
1 tsp. paprika
1 tsp. instant coffee
  powder
1 tsp. garlic powder
1 tbsp. brown sugar

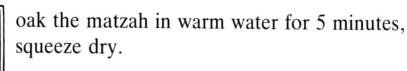

oak the matzah in warm water for 5 minutes, squeeze dry.

Saute the onion in the margarine, and mix with all the stuffing ingredients. Stuff the chickens.

Mix the soy sauce, the paprika, the coffee, the garlic and the brown sugar with ¼ cup of water. Brush the chickens with this glaze.

Roast for an hour at 375°. Baste frequently.

CHINESE CHICKEN OMELETTE

Leah Meron has imported this dish from her parents' home in Harbin, China.

Serves 6

4 eggs, separated
1 garlic clove, minced
1 tsp. ground ginger
½ lb. cooked or canned
  chicken meat
2 tbsp. soy sauce
1 tsp. sugar
2 tbsp. chopped
  scallions
Salt and pepper
4 tbsp. oil for frying

eat the egg whites until stiff peaks are formed.

Mix all the other ingredients, except the oil. Fold the egg whites gently into the mixture.

Heat two tablespoons of the oil in a large frying pan, and add half of the egg mixture. Fry until golden brown on both sides.

Repeat with the remaining mixture and serve immediately, sprinkled with drops of sesame oil.

GLAZED CHICKEN WINGS ON A MATZAH BED

Serves 6

5 matzah
3 eggs
Salt, pepper
Abt. 20 chicken wings

For the glaze:
1 tsp. garlic powder
4 tbsp. oil
⅓ cup water
1 tsp. paprika
4 tbsp. honey
1 tbsp. maple syrup

Break the matzah and cover with warm water, let stand for 5 minutes and squeeze dry.

Mix the matzah with the eggs, the salt and the pepper. Grease a heat–proof dish and line with the matzah mixture.

Cut each wing apart at the joints; discard wing tips or save to use in soup. Mix all the glaze ingredients. Arrange the wings on the matzah bed and brush them with the glaze.

Roast for an hour in a medium–high oven. Baste frequently and turn the wings once after 30 minutes.

PASSOVER HAMMIN

Serves 8

2 onions
10 small potatoes
2 small carrots
1 lb. chicken gizzards
1 small chicken, cut in
   eight pieces
Salt to taste
2 dates
2 oz. chicken fat or
   margarine
1 tbsp. sugar
Passover kugel
   (optional)

Hammim, a slowly cooked stew of meat, beans, barley and potatoes has enjoyed a startling revival in Israel in recent years. Hammin (or chulent) used to be a dish that older generation mothers and grandmothers cooked and the younger generation ate. There was a clear division of labor.

An invitation to a Hammin lunch on a winter Saturday was both common yet envied. But we never publicly boasted about our secret passion for this dish which practically contradicts all the rules of gourmet cooking. Recently, the Hammin lovers in Israel have begun to emerge from their closets – only to discover thousands of other kindred souls. Now, we not only eat it. We're all cooking it.

The ritual is the same whether your grandmother came from Lodz, Istanbul or even Brooklyn. It begins on Friday when the ingredients are all gathered and sealed in a heavy casserole. The casserole then goes into the oven at the lowest possible temperature and the magic begins. The aroma begins to infiltrate the other rooms of the house and by Saturday morning it has established an almost palpable presence.

This is when the neighbors start noticing it and begin dropping in for short visits – holding a plate. Well before lunch the sealed casserole is quietly opened and a fork is sneaked in and returns with its reward: a potato, a piece of kugel or a brown Hammin egg. I have yet to meet a family who could withstand the temptation and wait until lunch for the unveiling ritual.

eel the onions and slice. Peel the potatoes and the carrots and put all the ingredients except the sugar in a large casserole. Cover with water.

Heat the sugar in a heavy saucepan until dark brown and caramelized. Pour immediately into the Hammin casserole. The caramelized sugar as well as the dates will enhance the deep tan color of the dish.

Bring the Hammin to a boil on the stove, add the kugel (see recipe), seal the casserole and bake in a 200° oven or on a Shabbath plate for 12 hours.

PASSOVER KUGEL

1 large potato, grated
½ cup potato starch
½ cup matzah meal
¼ cup oil

1 large onion, grated
1 tsp. salt
1 egg

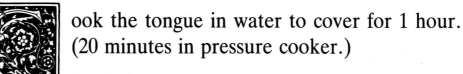

Knead all the ingredients by hand or in a food processor with a plastic blade.

Form one or two long loaves and add to the Hammin after the first boiling.

SWEET AND SOUR TONGUE

For this dish, try to find fresh beef tongue which has not been corned or marinated.

Serves 4–6

3 lbs. beef tongue
2 cups red cooking wine
3 bay leaves
Salt to taste
5 tbsp. apricot jam

3 tbsp. honey
3 tbsp. cider vinegar
½ cup raisins
Salt to taste

Cook the tongue in water to cover for 1 hour. (20 minutes in pressure cooker.)

Peel the tongue and pour off the cooking liquids. Add the wine, the bay leaves and all the remaining ingredients and cook for another hour, or until the tongue is very tender.

Remove and discard the bay leaves. Take the tongue out and chill. When the tongue is cold, slice it thinly and heat the slices in the sauce.

LAMB CHOPS IN PRUNES AND ONIONS

Serves 6

3 lbs. shoulder lamb
chops
4 large onions
1 cup raisins
½ lb. prunes
1 cup white cooking
wine
1 tbsp. honey
½ tsp. salt

hop the onions coarsely. Arrange the chops in an oven–proof dish. On top of the chops and in between them put the onions, the raisins and the prunes.

Mix the wine with the honey and the salt and pour over the meat, the fruits and the vegetables.

Cover the dish with aluminum foil and bake in a 350° oven for an hour.

Remove the foil and bake for another 40 minutes or until the chops are glazed and tender. Baste frequently.

Transfer the chops to a serving dish, arrange the prunes on the sides, heat the sauce briefly and pour over the chops.

LEMON VEAL WITH ARTICHOKES AND OLIVES

This dish is cooked easily and quickly in a pan. It is best prepared with the cracked, slightly bitter olives, pickled in olive oil and found in Arab or Mideastern food stores. If these olives are not available, use small green olives.

3 lbs. veal steaks
½ cup potato starch
¼ cup olive oil
½ cup green olives,
  pitted
10 canned artichoke
  hearts
Salt and pepper
3 tbsp. chopped parsley
½ cup white cooking
  wine
2 lemons

ust the veal steaks with potato starch and saute them in the olive oil in a large pan. When steaks are browned on both sides (about 3 minutes for each side), add the olives, the artichoke hearts, the salt, the pepper, the parsley and the wine.

Cover and simmer for at least 30 minutes on a low heat.

Add the juice of one lemon to the veal and simmer for 5 minutes. Cut the other lemon into wedges for garnish.

PASTELICOS WITH SPICY MEAT FILLING

Yield: 15 pieces

2 cups mashed potato
  flakes
3 eggs
3 tbsp. potato starch
½ tsp. salt
Ground black pepper
  to taste

For the filling:
1 large onion, chopped

4 tbsp. oil
1 lb. ground beef
½ tsp. salt
½ tsp. cumin
½ tsp. turmeric
½ tsp. paprika
2–3 drops of Tabasco
  sauce (optional)
2 eggs, beaten
Oil for deep frying

 ix the mashed potatoes with the eggs, the starch, the salt and the pepper. Refrigerate for 20 minutes.

Saute the onion in the oil. Add the ground meat and all the spices and cook for 20 minutes, stirring the mixture with a fork very frequently.

Put a little oil on the palms of your hands and shape the potato mixture into balls. Flatten the balls between both hands.

Put ½ tbsp. of meat filling on the dough , fold the edges of the dough over the filling and pinch to seal the edges.

Dip the pastelicos in the beaten egg and deep fry for 2 minutes on each side. Drain on paper towels.

PASSOVER SHEPHERD'S PIE

This dish uses meat and vegetable leftovers.

Serves 4

1 large onion, chopped
2 tbsp. margarine
2 cups cooked turkey,
  beef or chicken
1–2 cups leftover
  vegetables
1 cup (10¾ oz)
  condensed chicken
  soup
4 matzah
2 eggs, beaten
Salt and pepper

aute the onion in the margarine in a large saucepan, until golden. Add the meat, the vegetables, the condensed soup, and cook for 3 minutes.

Cut every matzah into four parts, sprinkle with a little water and let stand for 10 minutes.

Pour the meat into a 10–inch pie plate. Arrange the matzah quarters on top of the meat mixture. Pour the eggs over the matzah and season with salt and pepper.

Bake for 20 minutes in a 350° oven and serve hot.

NONA RACHELLE'S MINA DE CARNE

Every Passover, my husband's grandmother, Rachelle Barouche, is in charge of this specialty.

Serves 6–8

6 matzah
4 tbsp. oil
1 large onion, chopped
1 ½ lb. lean ground
  beef
⅓ cup chopped dill
Salt and pepper
1 cup prepared mashed
  potato flakes
4 eggs, beaten
½ tsp. salt

prinkle the matzah with water, put them one on top of the other and wrap with a damp towel.

Heat the oil in a large skillet and saute the onion. Add the meat, the dill, the salt and the pepper and cook for 15 minutes, stirring frequently.

Mix the potato puree with the eggs and the salt. Add a third of the mixture to the meat.

In a 9 inch square oven proof dish arrange alternating layers of meat and matzah, finishing with a matzah.

Spread the remaining potato mixture on the matzah and bake at 350° for 1 hour.

MEAT–LEEK KEFTIKAS WITH FRESH TOMATO SAUCE

Yield: 15 patties

1 large leek
1½ lbs. lean ground
  beef
3 eggs
1 tsp. salt
2 tbsp. matzah meal
Oil for frying

For the sauce:
2 tbsp. oil
2 large, ripe tomatos,
  diced
Juice of 1 lemon
Salt and pepper
1 tbsp. sugar
1 tbsp. chopped dill

Clean the leek and cut into slices. Cover with boiling water and cook for 10 minutes.

Drain the leek and mash with a potato masher or in a food processor.

Mix all the ingredients and shape into large patties. Fry the patties in hot oil on both sides until brown. Drain off excess fat.

In a separate saucepan, mix all the sauce ingredients and bring to a boil. Pour over the patties and cook for 10 minutes, uncovered.

LEEK PATTIES IN LEMON DILL SAUCE

For the patties:
See previous recipe

For the sauce:
2 cups water
Juice of 1 lemon.
1 tsp. sugar
3 tbsp. chopped dill
2 green peppers, sliced
1 tbsp. instant chicken
   soup

Combine all the sauce ingredients in a saucepan and bring to a boil.

Form small patties with wet hands and drop them in the sauce. Cook, uncovered, for 20 minutes and serve hot.

וְנָשַׁךְ לְשׁוּנְרָא · דְּאָכְלָה לְגַדְיָא
אַבָּא בִּתְרֵי זוּזֵי ; חַד גַּדְיָא · חַד גַּדְיָא
דָם הָאט גיקויפֿט : דֶּר הָאט גֶגֶעטֶין דֶמֶ דָם קֶעצְלַיְין
· מַיְין צִיקְלַיְין · מַיְין צִיקְלַיְין ·

· וְהִכָּא לְכַלְבָּא · דְּנָשַׁךְ לְשׁוּנְרָא · וְחַד גַּדְיָא · וְחַד
· דְּזַבִּין אַבָּא בִּתְרֵי זוּזֵי ; דֶר הָאט גֶבִּיטִין דֶמְטֶ קֶעצְלַיְין · דֶמְטֶ דָם ה
דֶּר הַאט גֶביסִין דֶם הַיְינְדְלַיְין · מוֹק צְווֵייא פֿפֿעֶמוֹטֶ מַיְין צִיקְלַיְין מַיְינֶ

· וְשָׂרַף לְחוּטְרָא · דְּהִכָּה לְכַלְבָּא ד · דְּאָכְלָה לְגַדְיָא · חַד גַּדְיָא · דְּזַבִּין אַבָּא בִּתְרֵי
זוּזֵי וְחַד גַּדְיָא חַד גַּדְיָא · דֶּר דָם הָאט גֶטוֹלְמֶין דֶמוֹ הַיְינְדְלַיְין ; דֶט
דֶר הַאט בְּרֶענְט דֶט טֶעצְקַיְין · דֶּט דֶם הַאט גֶגֶעטֶין דֶמוֹ צִיקְלַיְין דֶלְטֶ דֶל הַאט גִיקוֹיפֿט מַיְינ
מוֹק צְווֵייא פֿפֿעֶמוֹג : מַיְין צִיקְלַיְין · מַיְין צִיקְלַיְין

· וּכְבָה לְנוּרָא · דְּשָׂרַף לְחוּטְרָא · דְּהִכָּה
· דְּנָשַׁךְ לְשׁוּנְרָא · דְּאָכְלָה לְגַדְיָא · דְּזַבִּין אַבָּא
בִּתְרֵי זוּזֵי · וְחַד גַּדְיָא · חַד גַּדְיָא
דֶּט וֶומְטֶרְלַיְין · מוֹק פֿר לֶעטֶ דֶמְטֶ פֿיְימֶרְלַיְין · דֶּט דֶם הַאט פֿר בְּרֶענְט דֶּט טֶעקְלַיְין
גֶטוֹלְמֶין · דֶּט הַיְיוְלַיְין · דֶּט דֶם הַאט גֶביסִין דֶּט קֶעצְלַיְין · דֶּט דֶם הַאט גֶגֶעטֶין
מַיְין לִיקְלַיְין · מוֹס צְווֵייא פֿפֿעֶנוֹג מַיְין צִיקְלַיְין

· וְשָׁתָא לְמַיָּא · דְּכָבָה לְנוּרָא · דְּשָׂרַף
· דְּהִכָּה לְכַלְבָּא · דְּנָשַׁךְ לְשׁוּנְרָא · דְּאָכְלָה לְגַדְיָא
· חַד גַּדְיָא

זאתא לְנוּרָא · וְשָׂרַט
דְּכָבָה · דִּשָׂרַף לְחוּ
לְשׁוּנְרָא · דְּאָכְלָה לְגַדְיָא
· גַּדְיָא ·

דָא קֶמֶ דֶּר טוֹהֶט : מוֹק טֶעכְטֶ דֶען
דֶּט דֶם הַאט פֿר לֶעטֶּ דֶּט פֿיְימֶרְלַיְין ;
גֶטוֹלְמֶין דֶּט הַיְינְדְלַיְין : דֶּט דֶם הַאט גֶבֶ
דֶּט דֶם הַאט גִיקוֹיפֿט מַיְין פֿעֶטֶרְלַיְי

זאתא מלאך המ
דְּשָׂתָא לְמ
לְתוֹרָא
דְּהִכָּה לְכַלְבָּא · דְּ
דְּזַבִּין אַבָּא בְּ

רָא קֶמֶ דֶּר מלאך האות ·
מֵייְ גֶטְרוֹקֶין דֶמוֹ וֶומֶּרְלַיְין ·
טֶעטֶקְלַיְין : דֶלוֹ דֶל הַאט הַ
הַאט גִיגֶעטֶין דֶט צִיקְלַיְין

זאתא ה
דְּשָׂחַט לְ
דְּהַבָּא לְנוּ
לְשׁוּנְרָא

דָא קֶמֶ לֶ
דֶּר דֶם הַ
לֶעטֶּ דֶּ
הַיְינְדְלַיְי

VEGETABLES

SWEET AND SOUR CELERY ROOT

A classic from the Sephardic kitchen The celery root cooked in this method is very delicate in taste. In fact, it tastes like artichoke hearts.

I remember many hardships trying to peel the celery roots. Then, one day, my husband's grandfather, Haim Morhaim, was invited for dinner. As he watched me struggle, he suggested calmly: "Why don't you slice it first and then peel it" And the struggle was over.

Serves 4

1 large celery root
3–5 carrots
4 tbsp. oil
3 tbsp. lemon juice
1 heaping tbsp. instant
  chicken soup mix
3 tsp. sugar

ash the celery root. Do not peel. Cut the root into ¼" slices and peel each slice, easily. Peel and slice the carrots as well

Put all the ingredients in a heavy saucepan, add half a cup of water and cook, covered, on low heat for 30 minutes.

Glaze with the thickened sauce in the pan and serve hot or cold.

TZIMMES WITH DUMPLINGS

3 carrots
1 cup matzah meal
2 eggs
¼ cup (½ stick)
  margarine
Salt and pepper
2 tbsp. oil
¼ cup sugar
Pinch of cinnamon

eel and dice the carrots

In a bowl, mix the matzah meal with the eggs, the margarine and a little salt. Form into two large dumplings.

Cook the carrots with 2 cups water, salt, pepper, sugar, cinnamon and oil.

Bring to a boil. Add the dumplings, cover and cook for 20 minutes over low heat.

Slice the dumplings and serve them with the carrots.

ORANGE APPLE TZIMMES

The orange marmalade provides a bitter–sweet flavor.

Serves 4

2 lbs. carrots, peeled
   and sliced
2 apples peeled and
   diced
1 cup water
½ cup orange
   marmalade
⅓ cup honey
⅓ cup margarine
Grated peel and juice
   of one orange
½ tsp. cinnamon
½ tsp. salt

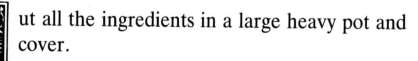 ut all the ingredients in a large heavy pot and cover.

Bring to a boil, lower heat and cook covered for one hour.

Remove the lid and cook for another twenty minutes, stirring occasionally until the carrots are glazed.

ARTICHOKE WITH THREE SAUCES

Fresh artichokes are at their best during the spring and can be enjoyed plain or with any of the following sauces.

Serves 6

1 large lemon
6 large artichokes
4 cups water
1 tsp. salt
1 bay leaf

ut off the artichoke stems.

Trim the tips of the leaves with a pair of sharp scissors. Cut the inner leaves with a sharp heavy knife.

Place the trimmed artichokes in a large pot, add the bay leaf, salt and lemon cut into wedges.

Cover and cook the artichokes for 40 minutes.

Drain and serve plain with lemon juice or with one of the following sauces.

SAUCE PILAR

Yield: 1½ cup

1 onion
1 cup mayonnaise
2 tbs chopped dill
1 tsp mustard
½ tsp salt
½ tsp paprika
1 tbs sugar

hop the onion in a food processor fitted with a steel blade. Add all the other ingredients and process just until mixed.

Keep refrigerated until used.

CAPER CREAM SAUCE

Yield: 2 cups

1 cup mayonnaise
¼ cup capers, drained
½ cup heavy cream
2 tbs mustard
2 tbs chopped parsley
1 tbs sugar
½ tsp white pepper

  ix the ingredients by hand and refrigerate.

WHIPPED HORSERADISH SAUCE

1 package (8 oz)
  whipped cream cheese
  at room temperature
½ cup white
  horseradish
1 tsp sugar
½ tsp salt
1 cup heavy cream

ix the cream cheese, horseradish sugar and salt together.

Whip the cream and fold gently into the cheese mixture.

Refrigerate.

GREEN BEANS IN MUSHROOMS

A simple yet very special combination.

Serves 4.

1 bag (16 oz) frozen
  green beans
½ lb. fresh mushrooms
¼ cup (½ stick) butter
  or margarine
salt and pepper

Cook the beans in 2 cups of water for ten minutes and drain thoroughly.

In the meantime, rinse the mushrooms and dry them in paper towels. Cut each mushroom in half and saute them in the butter for about ten minutes or until golden.

Add the beans, season with salt and pepper and cook for five more minutes. Serve immediately.

CAULIFLOWER BROCCOLI BOUQUET

A festive, beautiful vegetable array that will enhance every meat dish in this book.
The vegetables are steamed only briefly to preserve their freshness and crispiness.

1 bag (16 oz) frozen
  broccoli
1 bag (16 oz) frozen
  cauliflower
2 packages (10 oz each)
  frozen Brussel sprouts
Salt and pepper to taste

ut the frozen vegetables in a steamer, sprinkle with salt and pepper and steam for ten minutes.

If a steamer is not available, steam the vegetables in a large pressure cooker in the following manner: pour two cups of water into the cooker, place an empty tuna can in the cooker, place a heat proof plate on the can and pile the vegetables on it. Sprinkle with salt and pepper, cover and cook for three minutes after pressure has built up.

Arrange the vegetables on a large serving plate in the form of a bouquet, with the cauliflower and broccoli florets serving as the flowers and the Brussel sprouts as the leaves.

LEEK IN GARLIC BUTTER

A real gourmet treat that is quick and easy to prepare. The butter may be replaced by margarine, making the leek a perfect accompaniment to all the meat dishes in this book.

1 large leek
2 oz. butter or
  margarine
4 garlic cloves, minced
salt and pepper to taste
½ cup light cream
  (optional)

iscard the dark green leaves of the leek and cut the leek open lengthwise (this will allow for better rinsing).

Rinse the leek thoroughly and slice into ¼ inch rings.

Saute the leek and the garlic in the butter for ten minutes. Season with salt and pepper and saute for five additional minutes.

Add the light cream, cook for one more minute and serve hot.

EIGHT VEGETABLE DUMPLING STEW

A vegetarian Passover feast.

Serves 6–8

2 onions
2 carrots
2 red peppers
2 tomatoes
2 ribs celery
1 cup fresh mushrooms
⅓ cup oil
1 package (10 oz)
  frozen green beans
1 package (10 oz)
  frozen yellow beans

1 can (6 oz) tomato
  paste
1 tbs sugar
1 tsp salt

For the dumplings:
2 eggs
1½ cups matzah meal
1 tsp salt
⅓ cup water
6 tbs oil

Slice the onions, carrots, peppers, tomatoes, celery and mushrooms.

Heat the oil in a large heavy pot, add the vegetables and saute for ten minutes.

Add the frozen vegetable, tomato paste, salt and sugar with one cup of water. Cover and cook for twenty minutes.

Mix the dumpling ingredients and form small dumplings with wet hands.

Use a wooden spoon to make small wells in the vegetable stew and drop the dumplings in carefully.

134 Cover and cook for an additional twenty minutes.

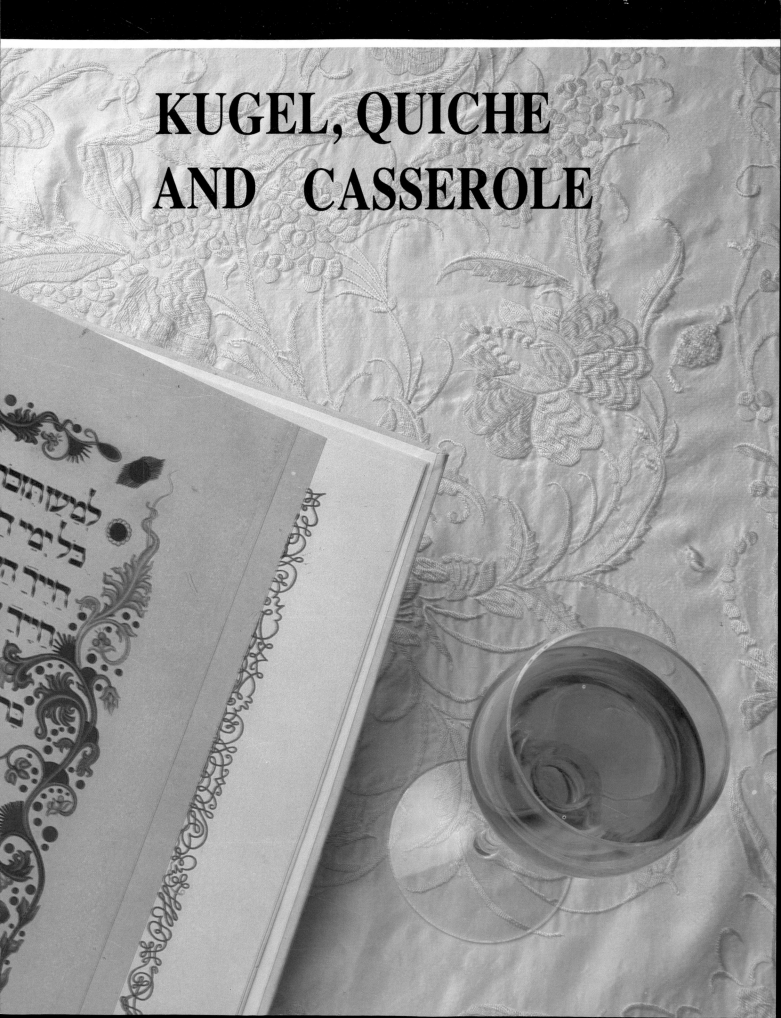

KUGEL, QUICHE
AND CASSEROLE

QUICK MICROWAVE BROCCOLI SOUFFLE

A quick dairy main dish.

Serves 6

2 tbs. butter
1 bag (16 oz) frozen
  broccoli
4 eggs, separated
3 tbsp. matzah meal
2 tbsp. chopped parsley
2 tbsp. chopped chives
½ tsp. salt
½ tsp. paprika
Salt and pepper
⅓ cup milk
½ cup grated parmesan
  cheese

Put the butter in a round 10 inch microwave dish and melt it at 'HIGH' for 1 minute.

Thaw the broccoli in the bag for 5 minutes in the microwave. Spread the broccoli pieces evenly in the buttered dish.

Beat the egg whites until stiff peaks form. Beat the egg yolks with the meal, the herbs, the milk and the spices.

Fold the egg whites into the mixture and pour over the broccoli. Microwave for 5 minutes at "HIGH" and allow the souffle to stand for another 5 minutes.

138   Sprinkle with the cheese and serve.

POTATO KUGEL

The food processor takes over and the long procedures of peeling and grating potatoes have turned into a very short and easy preparation.

Serves 6

5 large potatoes
2 onions
1 stick margarine
3 eggs, beaten
½ tsp. salt
½ tsp. black pepper

eel and grate the potatoes and the onions using the fine shredding disc of a food processor.

Melt the margarine and mix with all the other ingredients.

Grease a 13 by 9 inch baking pan, pour the mixture in and cover tightly with a lid or aluminum foil.

Bake at 325° for 1½ hours. Remove the foil and bake for another hour, or until golden brown.

OVERNIGHT CARROT–APPLE PUDDING

This is supposed to be a side dish, but after an entire night of slow cooking the pudding is brown and very aromatic, and in most cases it does not survive until meal time.

8 carrots, peeled and
  grated
3 apples, peeled and
  grated
1 cup raisins
½ cup chopped walnuts
½ cup diced candied
  orange peel
4 eggs
1 cup matzah cake meal
⅔ cup oil
1 cup brown sugar
¼ cup brandy
1 tsp. cinnamon
1 tsp. salt
½ tsp. ground ginger
½ tsp. allspice

ix all the ingredients in a large bowl.

Grease two loaf pans and divide the mixture between them.

Cover tightly with aluminum foil and bake at 325° for 30 minutes.

Reduce the heat to 150° (or lowest setting) and bake overnight, or at least 8 hours.

POTATO – YOGURT CAKES

A tasty accompaniment for fish, or a light meal in itself.

Yield:12 cakes

3 potatoes
2 onions, grated
2 oz. butter
2 tbs. chopped dill
½ tsp. salt
½ tsp. pepper
3 tbs. potato starch
2 eggs
2 cups plain yogurt

eel, slice and cook the potatoes for 20 minutes. Drain.

Saute the onions in the butter until golden.

Mash the potatoes and mix with all the remaining ingredients. Make sure the butter in which the onions were sauteed is incorporated in the mixture.

Grease a 12–muffin tin and heat in a preheated oven for 5 minutes.

Divide the potato mixture between the muffin cups and bake at 325° for 45 minutes or until golden brown.

ONION – YOGURT PIE

An easy, golden–brown no–crust pie, with a great onion flavor.

4 large onions
1 tsp. sugar
¼ cup (½ stick) butter
  or margarine
2 tbs. potato starch
3 eggs
2 cups plain yogurt
3 tbs. onion soup or dip
  mix

hop the onions and saute with the sugar in the butter for 10 minutes or until golden–brown.

Add the soup mix and the potato starch and stir for 2 minutes.

Remove from heat. Add the eggs and the yogurt.

Grease a 10 inch pie plate and bake at 350° for about 40 minutes or until golden–brown.

ESTHER'S ZUCCHINI FRITADA

1½ lbs. fresh zucchini
1 onion
3 tbs oil
5 matzah
1 cup cottage cheese
1 tsp salt
5 eggs
1 cup sour cream
1¼ cups (5 oz.) grated
  cheddar cheese

Fritada is a vegetable and egg pie unique to the Sephardic kitchen. The most common Fritadas contain spinach, leek or Swiss chard and are prepared in a large flat pan. Among the Turkish and Greek Jews, the Fritada has a special association with Pesah. A leek Fritada, "prasafuchi," is traditionally served as an appetizer at the night of the the seder and spinach Fritadas are served with breakfast all week long. Possibly as a result of this association Fritadas are prepared with Matzah all year round, lending something of the festiveness of the passover holiday to breakfasts and dinners at other times of year.

Eating Fritada has also become something of a ritual. Every family has its own way of eating Fritada and is surprisingly intolerant of other variations. In one home it will be eaten as a pie, with a knife and fork; in another it will be held like a slice of pizza. One family eats the Fritada with sour cream or yogurt while another uses lemon and a third, the purists, would consider it an insult to add anything. In most modern families the zealousness has been replaced by a willingness to try all methods.

My mother–in–law has extended the art of Fritada cookingto include a large variety of vegetables and in general has prepared the finest Fritadas I have ever tasted.

eel and grate the zucchini and onion and saute them in the oil for ten minutes.

Break the matzah, soak them in warm water for 5 minutes and squeeze them dry.

Mix the zucchini, onion and matzah with all the other ingredients.

Grease a 13 by 9 inch baking pan, spread the mixture evenly with moist hands and bake at 350° for about 50 minutes or until golden brown.

Serve with yogurt, sour cream or lemon juice.

145

LAYERED MUSHROOM CREPE BAKE

A very elegant main dish

For the crepes:
 cup milk
½ cup fine matzah meal
½ cup potato starch
3 eggs
½ tsp salt
1 tsp sugar
2 tbs melted margarine

For the mushroom filling:
3 onions, sliced thinly
2 tbs. butter
10 oz mushrooms,
 (fresh or canned)
1 tbs potato starch
½ cup milk

½ tsp salt
For the gratin:
1 cup heavy cream
2 eggs

Mix all the crepe ingredients in a blender or food processor until smooth.

Grease a crepe pan and make thin crepes. The pan should be greased only once before frying the first crepe.

Prepare the filling: Saute the onions in the butter for five minutes.

Slice the mushrooms and add them to the onions and saute them for another 5 minutes. Add the potato starch and stir.

Add the milk and stir until the mixture is thick and smooth and then remove from heat.

Grease a 12 inch pan and line it with 3 crepes. Spread a third of the mushroom filling over the crepes and keep layering crepes and filling ending with a layer of crepes on top.

Beat the cream with the eggs and pour it over the crepes. Bake it at 350° for 35 minutes or until the cream and egg mixture on top has set and turned golden brown.

LEEK GRATIN

The matzah are used to line the pan for the leek and the cream.

1 large leek
¼ cup (½ stick) butter
½ tsp salt
½ tsp ground pepper
¼ tsp nutmeg

1 cup heavy cream
5 eggs
2 matzah
1 cup grated cheddar
  cheese

Discard the dark green leaves of the leek and cut leek open lengthwise (this will allow for better rinsing).

Cut the leek into thin rings and saute in the butter for 15 minutes.

Add the salt, pepper and nutmeg.

Mix the eggs with the cream.

Break the matzah, soak in one cup of warm water for 5 minutes and squeeze dry.

Mix the matzah with a third of the cream and egg mixture and add a pinch of salt.

Grease a 10 inch pan and line the bottom with the matzah mixture.

Mix the leek with the remaining egg and cream mixture. Add the cheese and spread over the matzah in the pan.

Bake at 350° for one hour or until the mixture sets and is golden brown.

MAHAMMAR – MOROCCAN VEGETABLE AND EGG MOLD

This velvety, colorful dish is a traditional Passover appetizer among the Moroccan Jews. It can also serve as a vegetarian main dish.

4 potatoes peeled
6 eggs
½ tsp salt
½ tsp black pepper
1 tbs instant vegetable
   soup mix
1 small red pepper
1 can (16 oz) peas and
   carrots
¼ cup oil
1 hard boiled egg

ook the potatoes until soft. Mash them with the eggs, salt, pepper and soup mix.

Dice the red pepper and drain the peas and carrots.

Mix the vegetables with the potato mixture.

Heat the oil in a loaf pan or in a 10 inch tube pan on the stove for 2 minutes. Pour half of the mixture in the pan and spread it evenly.

Arrange slices of hard boiled eggs on top of the mixture and top it with the remaining mixture.

Bake at 350° for 50 minutes or until golden brown.

150   Allow to cool. Slice and serve at room temperature.

SPINACH GNOCCHI

The traditional gnocchi semolina is replaced by potato starch, but the results are still remarkable.

2 pkgs. (10 oz each)
  frozen leaf spinach
1 cup Ricotta cheese
1 cup grated Parmesan
  cheese
½ cup potato starch
2 egg yokes
Dash of nutmeg
½ tsp salt
5 tbs melted butter
½ cup grated Parmesan
  cheese

haw the spinach and squeeze dry.

Mix the spinach with the Ricotta, 1 cup Parmesan, egg yolks, potato starch, nutmeg, salt and pepper.

Boil three quarts of water with one teaspoon of salt.

Make small patties out of the mixture and ease them carefully into the boiling water. When the patties rise to the surface, they are ready.

Butter an oven–proof dish and arrange the Gnocchi inside without overlapping. Top with the melted butter and sprinkle with the Parmesan. Bake at 350° for about 15 minutes.

Serve plain or with the Three Cheese Sauce that follows.

THREE CHEESE SAUCE FOR GNOCCHI

This is my version of the famous Italian pasta sauce made with commonly available cheeses.
Instead of gratineed, the Gnocchi may be served with this rich sauce. Remove the Gnocchi from the boiling water with a slotted spoon, transfer them to a serving bowl and pour the creamy sauce over them.

4 tbs butter
3 oz blue cheese
1 tsp sugar
2 1–oz. wedges of
processed cheese
½ cup milk
⅓ cup grated Parmesan
cheese
Salt and pepper to taste

elt the butter in a deep saucepan. Crumble the blue cheese and add it to the butter. Stir vigorously.

Add the sugar and the processed cheese. Stir until the cheeses are completely melted. Add the milk and the Parmesan cheese and continue cooking, stirring constantly until the cheeses are well blended into the sauce.

Taste and add salt and pepper if needed.

154   Pour over the Gnocchi and serve immediately.

ESTHER'S SWISS CHARD FRITADA

A very tasty non dairy Fritada which can be served as an appetizer at a meat meal.

2 lbs. Swiss chard
3 tbs margarine
5 matzah
5 eggs
1 tsp salt
½ tsp pepper

Rinse the Swiss chard thoroughly and discard the white stems.

Cut the Swiss chard leaves into strips and saute them in the margarine for ten minutes stirring them frequently.

Break the matzah and mix them with the Swiss chard while it is still warm and let the mixture stand for about 5 minutes.

Add the eggs, salt and pepper.

Grease a rectangular, 13 by 9 inch long baking pan, spread the mixture evenly with moist hands and bake at 350° for 50 minutes or until golden brown.

PASSOVER BAGELS

There is no reason to give up lox and bagels on passover.

Yield: 8 bagels

2 cups water
1 tsp salt
1 tbs sugar
⅓ cup oil
2 cups fine matzah meal
4 eggs

Put the water, salt, sugar and oil in a large saucepan and bring to a boil.

Add the matzah meal at once, stirring vigorously. Remove from heat and let it cool for 5 minutes.

Fold the eggs into the dough one after the other and stir after each addition until the eggs are thoroughly blended.

Allow the dough to cool for one hour. Form long rolls of dough with moist hands and pinch the ends together into rings.

Arrange the bagels on a greased cookie sheet and bake at 325° for about 30 minutes or until the bagels are golden.

פרופס 60

CAKES AND
DESSERTS

במרום
שתהי למשמרת שלום, ישענו,
יי וצדקה מאלהי אלהים וא
ושכל טוב בעיני יום שכל
הרחמן הוא לחיי העולמים
ומטוחה, ינחילנו שכ
הוא ינחילנו ליום יזכ
המשינ הרחמן

CREAM CHEESE APRICOT CAKE

Serve it warm with vanilla ice cream.

4 matzah
1 cup sweet wine
5 eggs, separated
1 cup sugar
1 cup dried apricots
½ cup hazelnuts
½ cup raisins
½ cup dried figs,
chopped
8 oz cream cheese
1 tsp vanilla

Crumble the matzah. Heat the wine and pour over the matzah. Let stand for 20 minutes.

Separate the eggs: Beat the egg whites until stiff peaks form. Add half the amount of sugar gradually.

Chop all the dried fruits and nuts in a food processor or in a meat grinder.

Mix the dried fruits and nuts with the egg yolks, matzah, cream cheese, vanilla, remaining sugar and egg whites.

Grease a 13 by 9 inch pan and bake at 325° for 50 minutes.

COCONUT EGG MOLD

This rich dessert originated in Brazil and features an unusual combination of coconut, egg yolks and cheddar cheese. No one will be able to guess the last ingredient by tasting this unusual specialty.

10 servings

4 cups flaked coconut
2 cups boiling water
5 egg yolks
1¼ cups sugar
2 tbs butter, softened
½ cup shredded mild
  cheddar cheese
Juice of ½ lemon

For garnish:
Blanched almonds
  (optional)

lace the shredded coconut in a large bowl. Pour the boiling water over the coconut. Mix and allow to stand for 30 minutes.

Beat the egg yolks with the sugar until creamy. Add the butter, coconut, cheddar cheese and lemon juice.

rease a ring mold, dust the bottom and sides with powdered sugar and pour the coconut mixture into it.

Cover the mold with aluminum foil and bake at 300° for 40 minutes or until a knife inserted into the custard comes out clean.

Release the edges with a sharp knife and unmold onto a serving plate. Chill thoroughly before serving. Garnish with almonds, if desired.

ORANGE CHOCOLATE ROLL

A special flavor is added with Israeli Sabra liqueur, but any other orange liqueur can be used.

10 servings

8 oz semi sweet chocolate	Juice and grated peel of 1 orange
6 eggs separated	2 cups whipping cream
½ cup sugar	4 tbs Sabra (or other orange) liqueur
3 tbs matzah meal	
2 tbs cocoa	

rease a 15 by 10 inch jelly roll pan and line it with wax paper.

Melt the chocolate over a very low heat and allow it to cool for 10 minutes.

Beat the egg whites and add the sugar gradually. Beat the egg yolks and add to the chocolate.

Add the cocoa, matzah meal, orange juice and peel and 2 tablespoons of the liqueur to the chocolate. Fold the egg whites into the mixture.

Spread into the jelly roll pan and bake at 325° for about 20 to 25 minutes.

Allow to cool in the pan for 10 minutes.

Invert the cake from the pan on a clean cloth towel sprinkled with cocoa. Peel of the wax paper, cool completely for about 30 minutes.

Whip the cream and add the remaining liqueur to the cream. Spread the whipped cream over the roll but leave some for topping.

Roll carefully and top with the remaining whipped cream.

EASY CHOCOLATE BONBONS

Yield: 48

1 can (14 oz.)
  sweetened, condensed
  milk
1 package (12 oz.) dark
  semi sweet chocolate
  pieces
6 tbs. cocoa
4 tbs. butter
4 tbs. brandy
¼ cup additional cocoa
  for coating

our the condensed milk into a saucepan, heat to boiling, lower the heat and cook for 7 minutes stirring frequently.

Add the chocolate, cocoa, butter and brandy. Cook for 5 additional minutes, stirring occasionally.

Allow to cool to room temperature. Form smal balls with moist hands.

Roll in cocoa powder and arrange in paper petit–fours.

Chill for at least two hours before serving.

AMARETTO CHEESE SOUFFLE

8 servings

1 cup sour cream
2 containers (8 oz.
  each) whipped cream
  cheese
6 eggs, separated
1 cup sugar
3 tbs. Amaretto liqueur
5 tbs. matzah cake meal
1 tsp. vanilla
Grated peel of 1 lemon
Whipped cream for
  topping (optional)

Beat the egg whites until stiff peaks form. Add the sugar gradually.

Beat the egg yolks with the cheese and the sour cream. Add the Amaretto liqueur, the matzah meal, the lemon peel and the vanilla.

Fold the egg whites into the cheese mixture.

Grease a 10 inch spring form pan and bake at 325° for 50 minutes.

Cool on a rack and remove from the spring form. Refrigerate for several hours before serving.

Sprinkle with some more of the Amaretto liqueur and top with whipped cream. (Optional.)

MATZAH-WINE ROLLS

My mother's version of this popular Eastern European Jewish dessert

8 matzah
1 cup sweet wine
8 oz semi sweet
  chocolate
½ cup milk
2 tbs. cocoa
1 cup sugar
3 tbs. brandy
1 tsp. instant coffee
  powder
2 sticks margarine

rumble the matzah and soak in the wine.

Melt the chocolate with milk, cocoa powder, sugar, brandy and coffee over very low heat.

Remove from heat and add the margarine. Stir until melted. Add the matzah to the chocolate mixture.

Divide the mixture in two halves. Shape each half into a long roll and wrap tightly in aluminum foil.

Refrigerate overnight, remove the aluminum foil and slice. Place in paper petit fours.

MERINGUE WITH LEMON CREAM

For the meringue:
3 egg whites
½ cup sugar

For the cream:
3 egg yolks
½ cup lemon juice
2 cups whipping cream
1 can (14 oz) sweetened
  condensed milk

Chocolate syrup for
  garnish

Beat the egg whites until stiff peaks form. Add the sugar gradually, beating constantly.

Grease a 13 by 9 inch pan and line with greased wax paper.

Bake the meringue at 250° for 1¼ hours. Cool completely.

Prepare the lemon cream: Whip the cream until very thick and fluffy. Add the condensed milk slowly while still beating. Beat in the egg yolks and the lemon juice.

Remove the wax paper from the meringue and cut the meringue in half.

Spread the lemon cream on one meringue half, top with the other half and top with chocolate syrup.

172   Freeze for at least 3 hours before serving.

RAISIN FRITTERS (CHREMZLE)

The small village where we live was founded in 1933 by German Jews, and some of their culinary traditions are still preserved. The Passover Chremzle are among them.
My grandmother used to make these fritters with ground walnuts, and sometimes would fry the same batter with no fruits at all. They come out delicious and are served for breakfast.

Yield: About 18

3 eggs, separated
⅔ cup matzah cake
  meal
4 tbs. dark raisins
¼ cup sugar
Grated peel of 1 orange
1 tsp. vanilla
Oil for deep frying
Powdered sugar for
  dusting

eat the egg whites with a pinch of salt until soft peaks form. Add ½ cup of the sugar gradually while beating and continue to beat until very stiff.

Mix the egg yolks with the remaining sugar, then stir in the matzah meal, raisins, orange peel and vanilla. Fold the egg whites into the batter.

Heat the oil in a deep skillet or in a dutch oven.

Drop tablespoonfuls of the batter into the hot oil, and fry on both sides until golden. Remove with a slotted spoon and drain on paper towels.

Dust with powdered sugar.

BABANATZA – WINE PUDDING

A dark, candy like sweet from the Sephardic cuisine. This particular version comes from Rhodes.

1 cup dried apricots
1 cup dark raisins
1½ cups sweet wine
6 eggs
1 cup sugar
½ cup honey
1½ cups matzah meal
1½ cups chopped
  walnuts

Soak the apricots and the raisins overnight in the wine. Drain, reserving the wine.

Grind the apricots and the raisins with the grating disc of a food processor or with a meat grinder.

Beat the eggs and mix with all the ingredients.

Grease a 13 by 9 inch pan. Spread the mixture inside evenly and bake at 325° for 1½ hours.

Allow to cool and cut into diamonds or squares.

ALMOND SPICE COOKIES

Yield: About 4 dozen cookies

⅔ cup oil
⅔ cup sugar
1 egg, beaten
½ cup white wine
½ tsp. allspice
¼ tsp. ginger
½ tsp. cinnamon
2 ½ cups matzah cake
  meal
1 cup blanched almonds

Cream the egg with the oil and the sugar in a mixer.

Add the wine, the spices and the matzah cake meal. Add the almonds and mix with a wooden spoon.

Chill the dough for 1 hour.

Roll out the dough between two sheets of wax paper, ⅛ inch thick.

Cut out round cookies, with a cookie cutter or with a glass. Pierce the cookies with a fork and bake at 350° for 10 minutes.

177

QUICK DATE-NUT DIAMONDS

A great idea of Molly Forman from Inwood, New York This dessert does not require any flour.

3 eggs
½ cup sugar
1 cup chopped walnuts
¾ cup chopped dates
Grated peel and juice
  of 1 orange

Beat the eggs with the sugar and mix with all the other ingredients.

Grease an 8–inch square baking pan and spread the mixture evenly inside it or line a muffin pan with paper baking cups. Fill the paper cupcakes up to ⅔.

Bake at 350°: 20 minutes for cupcakes and 30 minutes for the square pan.

178

BIMUELOS: MATZAH CUPCAKES

Try these for a Passover brunch.

1½ cups crumbled
  matzah
4 eggs, beaten
¼ cup milk
½ tsp. salt
1 tbs. oil
1 tbs. sugar

oak the matzah in warm water for half an hour and squeeze them dry.

Mix with the remaining ingredients.

Grease a 12–muffin tin and fill it up to ⅔ of its depth.

Bake at 350° foor 45 minutes.

Serve with butter and various preserves.

STRAWBERRY MOUSSE

Serves 6

Serves 6

1 pint strawberries,
  washed and hulled
⅔ cup sugar
1 cup whipping cream
  or parve cream
⅓ cup boiling water
1 envelope unflavored
  gelatine
2 eggs, separated

Replace the cream by parve cream and enjoy this dessert at the end of a meat meal.

uree the strawberries with the sugar in a blender or a food processor.

Pour the boiling water over the gelatine and stir until the gelatine is dissolved. Add the gelatine to the strawberries and blend briefly.

Beat the egg whites until soft peaks form. Add the strawberry mixture and stir until combined.

Whip the cream and fold into the strawberry mixture. Pour into wine goblets and refrigerate until set.

STRAWBERRY WATER ICE

Serves 4

1 pint strawberries,
  washed and hulled
1 cup water
⅔ cup sugar
2 tbs. lemon juice
3 tbs. Grand Marnier,
  or other orange
  liqueur.

A refreshing non–dairy dessert

ut the strawberries, water, sugar, orange liqueur and lemon juice in a blender or a food processor fitted with a steel blade. Blend until smooth.

Freeze the strawberry mixture in ice trays for 2 hours.

Return the strawberry mixture to the food processor. Process until smooth and light in color.

182   Freeze again until serving time.

PASSOVER GRAPE PUNCH

Chill all the ingredients and combine them before serving.

Serves 10–12

2 cups Club Soda
2 cups orange juice
Juice of 2 lemons
6 cups grape juice
2 cups sweet red wine
1 can crushed pineapple
1 orange, sliced
Sugar to taste

ix all the ingredients in a large punch bowl, including the juice of the canned pineapple.

Add about 10 ice cubes and serve.

CARROT COMPOTE

This unusual, delicious and refreshing compote was created in Israel during the years of Austerity, when fruits, fresh as well as dried, were expensive and scarce. The Israeli cooks devised some very original and tasty compotes of carrots and zucchini. Their taste is so different that I let my dinner guests guess the ingredients. They never succeed but they love it anyway.

The carrots can be replaced by zucchini, for an equally delicious compote.

Serves 6

3 medium carrots,
  peeled and grated
5 cups water, divided
¾ cup sugar or the
  equal amount of
  artificial sweentener
½ cup lemon juice
Grated peel of 1 lemon
2 tbs. potato starch
1 tsp. vanilla

ook the carrots in 1 cup water for 20 minutes.

Add the sugar, lemon peel and 4 cups of water. Bring to a boil.

Mix the potato starch with ⅓ cup water and add it to the carrots, stirring until the potato starch is blended.

Cook for 2 more minutes, remove from heat and let cool.

Add the lemon juice and the vanilla. Refrigerate.

186   Serve cold.

INDEX